Contents

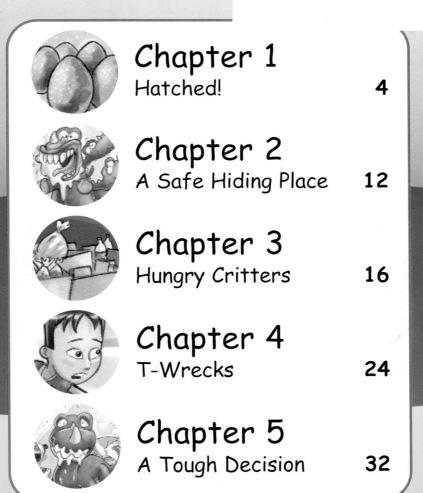

Chapter 1

Hatched!

Joseph and Sara were tired of swimming.

"Let's look for shells washed up near the cliffs," suggested Sara.

Joseph wasn't really interested in looking for shells because Sara always found the best ones. But he did like rocks, so he ran after her. When he reached the cliff, he saw that part of it had collapsed.

Near a big newly fallen boulder, Joseph found a
group of small, round rocks. Pointed at one end,
they were all the same colour.

'Almost like eggs,' he thought as he bent to pick
them up. He could hear a faint, hissing sound.
'Must be a crab somewhere near,' thought Joseph.

"Come on, you two," yelled Mum from the beach. "Time to go. The sun's getting too hot."

Joseph picked up the last of the special rocks and scrambled over to Sara.

"Look at my spiral shell," she said. "What've you got there?"

"Dinosaur eggs," said Joseph. He didn't know where the idea came from, but once he said it, he knew he was absolutely right.

"Don't be stupid," said Sara. As they walked across to Mum she added, "Can I have one?"

"No," said Joseph. "I've only got seven. They probably won't all hatch. Mum, can I have a bag for my dinosaur eggs?"

"Use the bucket," said his mother.

When they got to the car Joseph carefully put his bucket of dinosaur eggs behind him. Mum asked, "Who wants an ice-cream?" and he was so involved trying to decide between a giant Jellywobble and a raspberry Spinglespangle that he forgot all about the eggs.

The dinosaur eggs stayed in the back of the car all that hot day. And the next. They were in the back of the car all through the heatwave. Three days later, just as Joseph was waking up, he suddenly remembered them. He raced out to the car.

What a sight! A small, dark green, lizard-like creature was balancing on top of the steering wheel. Another had chewed a large lump out of the back of the front seat and was choking on pieces of foam rubber. A third squeaked as it swung from the rear-vision mirror, and a fourth was spluttering bits of the red, plastic bucket all over the seat. As Joseph watched, another lolly wrapper fell from the open glove compartment to join the pile of chewed paper on the front seat.

Joseph was horrified, but he couldn't open the door. How was he going to catch them all?

He had a brainwave and rushed inside. As he grabbed the Ricesnax from the breakfast table, Sara said, "Hey, I was just going to have some of those."

"Sorry Sara" Joseph said, as he grabbed a big jam jar from the cupboard. "Listen, those dinosaur eggs have hatched — give us a hand will you?"

Sara was open-mouthed when she saw what the hungry, baby dinosaurs were doing. But she helped Joseph as he carefully opened the door and caught them, one by one. She even managed to catch one by its tail as it disappeared under the car chasing a beetle.

Finally, Joseph and Sara had five small, green dinosaurs safely screwed into a jam jar. They were all crunching contentedly on Ricesnax.

Chapter 2

A Safe Hiding Place

Two of the dinosaur eggs hadn't hatched. As Sara and Joseph cleaned out bits of creamy-coloured eggshells, handfuls of foam rubber and a mass of sticky, chewed lolly wrappers, Sara asked, "So, what are we going to tell Mum?"

They both sighed. Mum always said dogs were too destructive to have as pets. After she saw the car she certainly wasn't going to be happy about pet dinosaurs.

For now, they had to find a safe place for the five small monsters.

"The garden shed?" asked Sara.

"How can we explain going down there all the time?" replied Joseph. "Besides, I want to watch them. Let's keep them under my bed."

It was relatively easy to smuggle the jar up the stairs and into Joseph's room. He put it on the warm windowsill.

"What sort of dinosaurs do you think they are?" asked Sara.

"Well, I know they're not big enough to be Tyrannosauruses," replied Joseph.

"Those little, spiky bits along their backs make them look a bit like Stegosauruses," said Sara thoughtfully. She had studied dinosaurs last year.

"But the horns on their noses make me think of Triceratops," said Joseph, not to be outdone. Miss Simmonds had been very pleased with his dinosaur project last term.

"There must be lots of dinosaurs that haven't been discovered yet," said Sara. "Do you think they're meat-eating or plant-eating dinosaurs?"

"Well, they've only eaten cereal and sweets and rubber and plastic so far," answered Joseph reasonably. "But their teeth are so sharp they can probably eat anything."

It turned out Joseph was right. About the only thing the baby dinosaurs couldn't get their teeth into was the glass of their jar.

Chapter 3

Hungry Critters

Joseph gave the dinosaurs toast, cheese, apple, salami and Weetsneeze. They enjoyed them all. They drank orange juice and milk, and liked fizzy drinks so much that one of them fell into the glass.

"It'll be all sticky now," said Sara when she stopped laughing and put it back in the jar.

"Don't worry," said Joseph. "Look." Two of them
were licking the one that had fallen in the fizz,
while it squirmed and squealed with delight.
The other two were sitting down, licking the
sticky liquid and squeaking happily. One of them
burped loudly.

"Joseph! Sara!" called Mum from downstairs.
"If you want to go to the supermarket with me
you'd better hurry up and clear this table."

"Oh dear," said Sara, and she and Joseph looked at each other.

"She doesn't know about the car yet," said Joseph glumly, and he hastily put the jar of dinosaurs under his bed.

"Careful," said Sara as she grabbed her sneakers. "We don't want them getting out."

"Goodness, you two did have good appetites this morning," said Mum. "We'll need some more Weetsneeze."

"And Ricesnax," added Joseph.

"And more fizzy drink and salami. And I think
we'll need lots of cheese." Sara was thinking
aloud. "Cheese is good for growing ... ah ... kids,
isn't it, Mum?" she asked innocently.

"Yes," said Mum in a puzzled voice. "Sara, is
there anything wrong?"

"We have to tell you about the car," interrupted
Joseph. "You know Tootsy from next door?"
Tootsy was the neighbour's poodle.

"The window was down and Tootsy must have got into the car," said Sara. "She made a pretty bad mess. We cleaned it up the best we could."

"Show me," said Mum, looking from one child to the other.

Her mouth fell open when she saw the holes in the upholstery.

"I don't know why on earth a dog would chew up the seat," she said. "The sweets, yes, but rubber?"

"It might have tasted of ice-cream," said Joseph.
"You know when Sara's Lollysplotch fell off her
stick the other day and melted all over the seat?"

"Don't remind me," said Mum. "Well, we can't really
say it was Tootsy's fault when we're not sure. I
suppose we'll just have to buy some car seat
covers. Jump in."

At the supermarket, Sara and Joseph persuaded
Mum to buy Frooty Loops and Chocosnaps, as well
as the Maltywheat biscuits that were on special.

"They need lots of carbohydrates," Sara whispered to Joseph. She was doing a unit on healthy eating at school.

"What about spinach, Mum?" asked Sara. Vitamins were important.

"Are you feeling all right, dear?" Mum inspected her.

"Have we got enough baked beans?" Joseph was thinking of the dinosaurs' enormous appetites.

"Get some more if you fancy them," said Mum. "Isn't it too hot for baked beans?"

22

There were four boxes of groceries to fit in the boot of the car instead of the usual two.

"You must be having a sudden growth spurt, both of you." Mum shook her head. She sighed again when she looked at the chewed seat. "Jump in."

Chapter 4

T-Wrecks

No-one spoke much on the way home. Joseph was trying to figure out how to smuggle baked beans up to the baby dinosaurs without Mum noticing. Sara was trying to work out whether they'd had enough protein today, and Mum was thinking of food bills and wondering about the cost of car seat covers.

Sara and Joseph helped Mum carry in the groceries.

They all saw the trail of eggshells, coffee grounds and potato peelings at the same time.

"Oh no, the dinosaurs! They've escaped!" gasped Joseph.

There, he saw a sea of shredded tissues. In the middle was an empty tissue box, slowly making its way through the tattered paper like an old boat. Excited squeaks came from inside it.

"I'll get this one," Sara yelled.

Joseph ran on, up the stairs, past Mum's bedroom. White powder drifted out, and a heavy, exotic scent hung in the air. "Mum's best perfume!" thought Joseph.

At first glance, his room seemed to have escaped lightly. All the books had been tipped onto the floor, and the baby dinosaurs had tried some Lego for morning tea. Nothing else was upset. Or was it?

What was happening in the fish tank? A small, green dinosaur was struggling in the water, a flapping goldfish in its mouth. Joseph hurriedly counted his goldfish. Where was the pair of bronze comets? He grabbed the overturned jar from the floor and heaved the dinosaur out of the fish tank, not very gently. It went snout first into the jar, still clutching the goldfish firmly in its pointy teeth.

There was a shriek from downstairs. What was going on down there? Joseph ran down the stairs two steps at a time, the baby dinosaur squeaking in protest.

Sara was shaking her hand. She put her thumb into her mouth and mumbled, "Bit me!" The sea of tissues rippled as the dinosaur escaped again.

Mum came into the room with a bandaid and stopped when she saw Joseph's jar.

"What are they?" she asked, staring. "Some sort of lizard?"

"Dinosaurs," Sara spoke round her thumb.

"Remember the eggs I found at the beach? I left them in the car," added Joseph.

"So that's what happened to the car." Mum nodded her head. "I knew it wasn't Tootsy. How many are there?"

"Five." Sara had her bandaid on now. "One in here, one in the kitchen ..."

"This one here," Joseph showed them the jar that now held one very fat dinosaur and no goldfish, "and two more upstairs."

"I'll get those ones," Mum decided.

Sara and Joseph had to pick up all the tissues before they could corner the slippery creature in the living room.

"He's fast, this one," panted Joseph as he lost him again. Finally, the baby dinosaur joined his fat, fish-eating brother in the jar, just as Mum came downstairs with her two.

"This little beast spilt all my talcum powder," she said grimly. "I followed the footprints in red nail polish across the carpet and found it in the closet."

Chapter 5

A Tough Decision

The baby monster in Sara's room was easier to catch.

"It was in Sara's dolls' cot," Mum told them, "eating the feeding bottle. Sara, I'm afraid it wrecked all your video tapes. It's like a jungle of brown tape up there."

"Oh," said Sara sadly. She loved her videos.

"That makes four," said Mum. "One more to go." They heard rustlings from the kitchen.

It was even worse than they feared. The dinosaur in the kitchen had found the box of fresh groceries on the floor. It had tried all the tubs of yoghurt, sampled the toothpaste and ripped open the flour.

Obviously it recognised the fizzy drinks, because it had punctured three bottles with its sharp teeth. Orange fizz was oozing under the fridge and lapping around the stove.

"And what on earth's that?" asked Mum, pointing to a frothy mess in the other corner. The new jumbo bottle of detergent lay on its side, and Joseph recognised Frooty Loops and lumps of peanut butter decorating a pile of Maltywheats in the middle of the suds.

The baby dinosaur had also sampled the Vegemite, before romping in the clean clothes in the laundry basket.

Mum set off across the kitchen with a jar and a determined look. She ended up flat on her back when she slipped over on the spilt soapflakes. An hour later they sat down at last, exhausted. Mum looked at the three bottles full of twisting, hissing, dark green terrors and then stared at the two boxes of ruined groceries.

"What are we going to do with them?" Sara asked.

"They can't stay here," said Mum. The children nodded. Even they could see that.

"But they're so cute!" said Joseph sadly. Mum smiled faintly as the fat dinosaur burped again.

"I'll ring the zoo," Mum said firmly.

The zoo was delighted. No other zoo had a baby dinosaur, let alone five. The family was given a free zoo pass, so they could go to see their dinosaurs anytime.

"I wish we could've kept them," Joseph said wistfully as they left. Mum looked at him and patted the new seat covers.

"Really?" she asked with a laugh.

Glossary

boulder
a big rock

growth-spurt
growing suddenly

lapping
gently splashing

ransacked
searched messily

romping
playing in an excited way

smuggle
to take secretly

spiral
something that winds around away from the middle

spluttering
quickly spitting out

upholstery
furniture covering

wistfully
thoughtfully

Wendy Blaxland

My favourite beach treasures are rocks the sea has rolled around in its mouth and polished with its big, green tongue. Some are perfectly round, others mottled or ringed. I call them 'dinosaur eggs' for fun. Now, I also own a tiny fragment of a real, fossilised dinosaur egg, bumpy all over. I know my 'dinosaur eggs' aren't real. But what if they were?

Steven Hallam